Spreading Kindness

Volunteering

by Brienna Rossiter

www.focusreaders.com

Focus Readers is distributed by North Star Editions:
sales@northstareditions.com | 888-417-0195

Produced for Focus Readers by Red Line Editorial.

Photographs ©: Shutterstock Images, cover, 1, 4, 7, 10, 14, 16, 18, 20; iStockphoto, 8, 13

Library of Congress Cataloging-in-Publication Data
Names: Rossiter, Brienna, author.
Title: Volunteering / by Brienna Rossiter.
Description: Lake Elmo, MN : Focus Readers, 2021. | Series: Spreading
    kindness | Includes index. | Audience: Grades 2-3
Identifiers: LCCN 2020033523 (print) | LCCN 2020033524 (ebook) | ISBN
    9781644938133 (hardcover) | ISBN 9781644938157 (paperback) | ISBN
    9781644938195 (pdf) | ISBN 9781644938171 (ebook)
Subjects: LCSH: Voluntarism--Juvenile literature. | Volunteers--Juvenile
    literature.
Classification: LCC HN49.V64 R664 2021 (print) | LCC HN49.V64 (ebook) |
    DDC 302/.14--dc23
LC record available at https://lccn.loc.gov/2020033523
LC ebook record available at https://lccn.loc.gov/2020033524

Printed in the United States of America
Mankato, MN
012021

About the Author

Brienna Rossiter is a writer and editor who lives in Minnesota. She loves cooking food and being outside.

Table of Contents

Chapter 1

You Can Help

Volunteers are people who help without being paid. There are many ways to volunteer. Some volunteers pick up trash. Others give food or clothes to people in need.

Some people go to areas where there has been a fire or storm. They help clean up and rebuild. But volunteers don't have to travel. You can help right in your **community**.

Examples of Volunteering

Join a cleanup group.

Help at the library.

Visit a nursing home.

Walk or run to raise money.

Chapter 2

Helping Others

Volunteers often help other people. Many volunteers cook. Others serve meals. The food goes to people who are going through hard times.

Other volunteers visit people who are sick or old. Some of these people cannot leave their homes. So, volunteers bring food. They bring supplies.

Volunteers can also talk to people or play games with them. They help people feel less **lonely**.

Help a Neighbor

Many volunteers help close to where they live. Think about what your neighbors might need. Do they have pets or plants that need to be cared for? Would they like help raking or shoveling? Could your family bring them **groceries**? Make a list of ideas. Then choose one way to help.

Chapter 3

Helping Animals

Some volunteers help animals. They might work at a **nature center** or zoo. These places take care of animals. Volunteers help feed the animals. They also clean cages.

Many volunteers help at animal shelters. These places care for animals that don't have homes. Volunteers can walk the dogs. They can hold rabbits or cats.

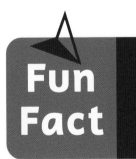

Fun Fact

Some volunteers care for animals in their homes.

Chapter 4

Helping Earth

Some volunteers help the **environment**. For example, some people plant trees. Trees help keep the air clean. They are also homes for animals.

Volunteers work to keep parks and rivers clean. Many volunteers work in groups. They pick up trash. They help keep Earth beautiful and healthy.

Fun Fact

Recycling is another way to help. People make less trash when they use things again.

FOCUS ON

Volunteering

Write your answers on a separate piece of paper.

1. Write a sentence describing the main idea of Chapter 1.

2. What kind of volunteering would you enjoy the most? Why?

3. What is one way you can help the environment?
   - A. cook a meal
   - B. pick up trash
   - C. give away clothes

4. How could playing a game help people feel less lonely?
   - A. People can play games all by themselves.
   - B. People can spend time together while they play.
   - C. People can stay far apart while they play.

Answer key on page 24.

Glossary

community
A group of people and the places where they spend time.

environment
The natural surroundings of living things.

groceries
Food that is sold at a store.

lonely
Feeling sad as a result of being alone.

nature center
A place that teaches people about the environment. It often has land where plants and animals can live.

recycling
Using an old item to make something new.

To Learn More

BOOKS

Gaertner, Meg. *Mark Gives Back: A Book About Citizenship.* Mankato, MN: The Child's World, 2018.

Huddleston, Emma. *Planting a Seedling.* Lake Elmo, MN: Focus Readers, 2021.

NOTE TO EDUCATORS

Visit **www.focusreaders.com** to find lesson plans, activities, links, and other resources related to this title.

Index

Answer Key: 1. Answers will vary; 2. Answers will vary; **3.** B; **4.** B